LIVE IT -
REALY LIVE IT!

*Your personal guide for getting
the most out of life!*

Tom Wendt

Spotlight Publishing

Spotlight Publishing
4202 Weatherstone Rd.
Crystal Lake Illinois, 60014

Live it-Really Live it! / Tom Wendt. -- 1st ed.
ISBN: 978-1-7320409-3-9
The Publisher has strived to be as accurate and complete as possible in the creation of this book.

This book is not intended for use as a source of legal, business, accounting or financial advice. All readers are advised to seek services of competent professionals in legal, business, accounting, and finance field.

In practical advice books, like anything else in life, there are no guarantees of income or results made. Readers are cautioned to rely on their own judgment about their individual circumstances to act accordingly.

While all attempts have been made to verify information provided in this publication, the Publisher assumes no responsibility for errors, omissions, or contrary interpretation of the subject matter herein. Any perceived slights of specific persons, peoples, or organizations are unintentional.

DEDICATION

I dedicate this book to everyone who knows there's more to life than they have experienced but are reluctant to reach beyond what they know.

I dedicate this book to anyone who has befriended fear more than they have befriended ability.

And lastly, I dedicate this book to all who are ready to aim high and rocket into the unknown. Rockets need guidance, I hope you find it in this book.

Table of Contents

INTRODUCTION

Within my mind, I often argue with and deny myself what I'm capable of or what's best for me. I sometimes find and buy into excuses that prevent me from moving forward in new ways like writing this book. I told myself that I didn't have the formal credentials I needed to write it. Fortunately, I wrote it anyway.

It seems to me that many authors of personal growth/self-help books write about their time spent in ashrams, climbing Machu Picchu, or obtaining an advanced degree.

Not me. In my younger days, my friends and I would make the rounds of redneck bars hustling pool.

Following such a night, driving home, as intoxicated with ourselves, as with the beers we had consumed, we would laugh at the patrons of the just-visited establishments. Obviously, in our minds, they weren't as smart as us or as well educated. They hadn't even applied themselves to finish high school, as we had. Oh yeah, we were so much better than them.

In hindsight, I realize that I was operating from a complete void of self-worth. My attempts at character assassination of others, was me coping with the endless, internal character assassination of myself. I was, as the Jackson Brown song says, *Running on Empty*.

And since I had little to distinguish myself and get the attention I so dearly craved, I got into owning fast cars. I felt important and powerful behind the wheel of a shiny, powerful vehicle. I am lucky to be alive. By deriving my self-worth from fast cars and drinking alcohol, I experienced a number of "close calls." I consider myself extremely fortunate to have never hurt others or myself with such reckless behavior.

Thus, too much of my education has been the knowledge and insights gained from taking foolish chances, acting out from my own immaturity and disrespecting others, but mostly, trying to be something I was not. I have a PhD. in that last one.

I am fortunate to have found the benefits of psychotherapy around the age of forty, which is when I began to mature. From there I found a Twelve-Step program and a spiritually oriented church. Thus, began my life of introspection and personal growth.

The ideas expressed in this book are mine, based on both personal experience and the teachings of others that I have managed to incorporate into my life. I stand behind them. Admittedly, I struggle to apply my own teachings consistently. So, while I don't always follow what I teach, I stand behind the teachings.

I extend my gratitude to author Price Pritchett, and Rev. Chris Chenoweth, whose writings inspired mine.

It is my hope that reading this book will encourage you to bring all you have to life, to take steps before you are ready, and to continually look within for lessons learned and potential possibilities.

Don't wait until you have the credentials to move forward. Just move forward in life.

Live it – Really Live it!

CHAPTER 1

IT BEGINS WITH ME

> *Self-care is never a selfish act - it is simply good stewardship of the only gift I have, the gift I was put on earth to offer others. Anytime we can listen to true self and give the care it requires, we do it not only for ourselves, but for the many others whose lives we touch.* Parker Palmer, *Let Your Life Speak: Listening for the Voice of Vocation*

You've decided to take a cross-country journey from Chicago, Illinois, to Los Angeles, California. Your desires are to meet people and see the sights along the way. You have four weeks to complete the trip. Two vehicles are at your disposal. Both provide adequate space for luggage and personal items. Cost is not an issue.

The first vehicle is 12 years old, has traveled 275,000 miles, and hasn't been subjected to regular maintenance. The brakes work but are badly in need of replacement. Sometimes the engine overheats. The tires are worn, and they too need replacement. Did I mention that the windshield is cracked?

The second vehicle registers 12,000 miles. Tires, brakes, and windshield are almost new. It runs perfectly.

Which vehicle would you choose for your trip? Vehicle #2? Good answer!

Now let's look at the physical, mental, emotional, and spiritual body that takes you on your life's journey. 24/7 it's what gets you around every day. Whether working, relaxing, socializing, exercising, loving, hating, growing, or remaining stagnant, this body of yours is your ride for the day. Your only ride. Every day, until it stops running.

What shape is it in? How's your maintenance program looking? Is your body unreliable and showing its age, perhaps appearing even older and with more miles than it actually has? Or, does it belie its age; healthy, in good repair, well rested and maintained, ready for the next stage of the journey?

Given the option, you wouldn't take a long, or perhaps even a short trip, in an unreliable automobile. Why would you take your life's journey in an unreliable body, mind, and spirit?

Your number one priority is Self-Care! Put yourself first, number one, numero uno! Only after that, with few exceptions, should you be setting out on your life's journey, or caring for others.

How long since your last physical exam? Mammogram? Colonoscopy? Prostate exam? Eye exam? Dental check-up?

a. About a year?

b. Three years?

c. Longer?

The correct answer for most is – A - about a year. Oh, it's been longer than one year? Stop reading this book and make an appointment for the physical exam you need...now!

You say you can't afford the time or money for a physical? OK, understood. Then you're choosing to live your life in Vehicle #1. Get ready for a breakdown. Did you know that a breakdown is far costlier in terms of time and money than a physical? Not to mention the damage it can inflict.

Also, unlike a physical exam, you can't schedule a breakdown. It just happens when it happens. Whether it's your auto or your body, breakdowns are far costlier than maintenance. Value yourself, schedule a physical!

> *Until you value yourself, you won't value your time. Until you value your time, you will not do anything with it.* M. Scott Peck, author, and speaker

Are there others counting on you? At home? At work? Where you volunteer? Somewhere else? Do you really want them relying on someone who is unreliable, capable of breaking down in the near future? Or are you willing to take the time for maintenance, and possibly repair, so that you're ready for the long-haul?

Schedule the physical you need. Now.

> *How you treat yourself is how you're inviting the world to treat you.* Unknown

CHAPTER 2

MAKE YOUR DAY

Live your life or it will live you. Unknown

Approach each day as though you are the ruler, the king, the queen; determining what will be and what won't be. Determine your schedule for the day. Even when there are others who are rightly dependent on you and need your attention, such as your children, your partner, your workmates, you determine the timing and attitude with which you will fulfill your responsibilities.

Back in the day when I was just a kid, and on those days when I actually believed that I had the right to speak my mind at home, (my parents were of the "children should be seen and not heard" mentality), the threatening response I often heard was, "You'd better watch your language, young man!"

> **Watch Your Language!**
> Mom and Dad

So, I entered adulthood reluctant to express my opinions and feelings. But that's a topic for another chapter, perhaps another book.

I suggest, however, that "Watch your language," continues to be good advice in terms of beginning and ending your day. If you start your day with "I have so much to do that I don't know how I'm going to get it all done," then you have set yourself up for a relatively miserable day, filled with stress and feeling overwhelmed.

Whether your words are spoken aloud or silently in the hallways of your own mind, they set the tone for the day and will likely be reinforced by your thought filters throughout the day. Most everything you encounter will be seen in ways that reinforce your initial assessment of the day to come.

If you retire at night reflecting on what a difficult day this has been, hoping that tomorrow will be better, but actually believing that it won't, guess what kind of day you'll have set up for yourself? You got it . . . a difficult one.

Watch your language and your actions. Make your day. Intentionally create customs and rituals by which to begin your day. Everyday. By taking the time to set an intention for the next 24 hours, the day you want to experience, you validate that this day, and how you live it, is important. As a result, your filter for the day, the manner in which you view and experience its events, will reflect the importance of creating the day you want.

So, if you're heading for an important job interview, first date, business meeting, social event, set yourself up to succeed in mind, body, and spirit. As inspirational speaker Les Brown says, "Show up looking good, feeling good, and smelling good." I'll add "thinking good."

Avoid the trap of wondering how it will go. Instead, imagine yourself succeeding. Vision the outcome you desire and make all your moves from that vision. How you began, your day will help determine your successful vision.

There are endless resources that will inspire you to begin your day in a fashion that supports having a good one. Books, videos, webinars, seminars, abound with information and suggestions, multi-step modalities, and specific actions to create your day. I'll let you do the research and create your own "begin the day" rituals. Creating such a plan will help you get the most out this book, but most importantly, your life.

Be grateful

Drink water

Journal

Shave

Brush teeth

Wash face

Take supplements

Exercise

Stretch

Breakfast

That's how I begin my day. I even have a check-off list to ensure that I don't forget. It works for me.

As you design your personal rituals, pay attention to the physical (exercise, hygiene, diet), the spiritual/ emotional (journaling, meditation, prayer, reflection), and your attitude (affirm it's going to be a good day, know that you can handle any challenges that arise). Consciously create a ritual to begin your day. Stay with it, repeat it daily. Make your day.

The same holds true for retiring at night. Create a sustainable ceremony of sorts, an observance of the day ending, in addition to a desirable vision of what tomorrow will bring. It need not be lengthy; its function is to set your consciousness, your attitude, for the next day, and for a good night's sleep.

If you're going to live your life, I mean really live it, then take control of the beginning and end of each day. Set yourself up to live intentionally.

> *Our intention creates our reality.*
> Wayne Dyer, author, and speaker

CHAPTER 3

FIND, AND FOLLOW YOUR BLISS

> *The saddest people I've ever met in life are the ones who don't care deeply about anything at all. Passion and satisfaction go hand in hand, and without them, any happiness is only temporary, because there's nothing to make it last.* Nicholas Sparks, *Dear John*

Now that you've created a firm foundation for a life that moves at the speed of imagination, by taking care of your physical body and emotional/spiritual well-being, let's continue moving forward.

While I was attending a morning networking group, the conversation turned to social media. One individual shared that too often when she attempts to send a tweet, she'll begin it, then delete it, begin again, delete, begin, delete. She said, "I just can't decide what I want to say."

As several members of the group nodded their heads in acknowledgment, I thought one member's response to her dilemma was spot on. "You don't know what to say because you don't have a strategy, a goal or a passion underlying your tweet." Like I said, "Spot on!"

How can we say what we want to say if we don't know what we want to say? How can we utter clear statements when we're unclear about what we want to state? The truth is until we have a purpose to what we say, what comes out is mishmash, random, unstructured thoughts that convey little, if any meaning.

The same holds true of our life experience. When we're unclear about what we want, when we lack a destination, when we haven't defined our goals and dreams, our passion and our bliss, then our journey is one of wondering and wandering. Directional lack of clarity leads us to a step forward, a step backward. We may survive, but we'll never thrive. I've heard it said, "There is no favorable wind to the sailor who lacks a destination."

Find and follow your bliss, your passion. What do you like to do? I mean, what do you **really** enjoy doing and experiencing? Define it. Vision yourself gleefully enjoying it. Then take a step in the direction of integrating it into your life.

If money and time were not an issue, here's what I would be doing:

1. _____

2. _____

3. _____

4. _____

> *Choose a job you love, and you'll*
> *never have to work a day in your life.*
> Anonymous

Fill in the blanks and feel free to create more blanks. Then begin taking steps in the direction of your bliss. Perhaps your first step will be internet exploring, gathering information and ideas. You might make a call to a resource. One option is to discuss your bliss with someone who will support your following it. Joining a supportive group could work, as a wanna-be author might join a writer's group.

I wish to make it clear that I am not suggesting you immediately quit your job, sell your house, end relationships, and such. What I am suggesting is, just as you "Make Your Day" as discussed in Chapter 2, by focusing on the kind of day you want, do the same with your life.

Focus on your bliss and follow it by taking steps in the direction of it. There's no need to concern yourself with the "how," that is, how you'll ultimately realize your bliss. That will unfold as you take steps in the direction of your passions.

> *Follow your bliss and the universe will open doors for you where there were only walls.*
> Joseph Campbell, author, and speaker

CHAPTER 4

AUTHENTICITY – BE YOURSELF

> *To be yourself in a world that is constantly trying to make you something else is the greatest accomplishment.*
> Ralph Waldo Emerson, essayist

I'm sitting at a family gathering, and a distant relative walks in with two friends. All three are heavily tattooed. It turns out that the three of them are tattoo artists. They are the creative souls who apply their skills such that, ultimately, a tattoo of one's desire is affixed on the body part of one's choice.

I've always struggled with tattoos. There's a part of me that wants to look closely and examine them, and there's a part of me that feels reluctant to do so. It seems intrusive to me, gawking at the artwork on another's body. Whenever I find myself in such a dilemma, where I want to do something, and at the same time, I'm telling myself not to do it, I experience a kind of creative tension in my gut. Anxiety. What should I do? Typically, I do nothing. Not a good choice. The next time a similar set of circumstances arise, I experience anxiety again...and again.

To me, that feeling is a red flag that some kind of action or reconciliation needs to occur. In this case, "What are the 'do's' when it comes to tattoos?" So, I explained my dilemma to one of the artists. "Should I look, should I not look?" Her answer was incredibly simple and obvious. "Ask them." That's it, "Ask them about their tattoos." Duh!

Following her advice, I asked her about a rather large one, running from shoulder to wrist. While admittedly disagreeing with some of her logic, I found her response intriguing. Most importantly, I asked. No tension, no anxiety, no wondering. What I experienced was a calmness and an interest in what she had to say. In my experience, that's what happens when I'm authentic, when I'm in integrity with myself and my thoughts. Be authentic, be yourself, and be calm. Lesson learned. When I'm curious, when I'm wondering what to do, be authentic...ask.

The same lesson can be applied to those times when I question myself. In the opening sentence of the introduction to this book I stated, "Within my mind, I often argue with and deny myself what I'm capable of or what's best for me." The best question I can ask myself in those cases is, "Why not?" The answer is typically a flimsy excuse that can be easily deconstructed, and then I move forward.

> *Authenticity requires vulnerability, transparency, and integrity.* Janet Louise Stephenson, author, and speaker

CHAPTER 5

WHEN THE UNTHINKABLE HAPPENS

My first daughter's stillborn twin; my mother-in-law's multi-year demise due to Alzheimer's; my first wife's diagnosis and ultimate death due to colon cancer at 40 years of age; my dad's suicide; the terrorism events of September 11, 2001; the news in general...

Following each of these events, I felt paralyzed. I recall seeing, and yet not seeing; hearing, and yet not hearing; feeling nothing and feeling everything. I recall a torrent of raw emotion flooding my entire being, so overwhelmed that I was practically unable to function.

I felt trapped in a pragmatic need to function in a world that continued to heap responsibilities upon me.

What is there to do when the "unthinkable" happens? What is mine to do when my emotional and intellectual pathways are short-circuited, seemingly non-functioning, as the result of "unthinkable" turns of events? How do I respond to my acute sense of powerlessness? How should I react when sorrow, or anger, or fear, holds a vice-like grip on me? And then, following the "unthinkable," an underlying sense of "Now what?" "What am I supposed to do?" "How do I take care of my family?" settles in.

What is one to do with all of that?

First - <u>Don't deny the difficulty in dealing with the event</u>

If you're hurting, honor the hurt. If you're angry, be angry. If the sense of loss and grief are overwhelming, admit it. Avoid the "someone has it worse than me" approach that wants to minimize your experience.

> *Our disaster personalities are far more*
> *complex and ancient than we think.*
> *But they are also more malleable.*
> Amanda Ripley, author

Hang in there, don't try to rush the recovery. For a while, be with the emotions you experience.

Second – Utilize community

Wherever and whenever you can, rely on others for support and assistance. Utilize the presence of family for reassurance, comfort, and compassion. Let them console you, as perhaps, you console them. Utilize your spiritual or faith community, your yoga group, your bike club, any community of which you are a part. Allow them to assist with meals, errands, child-care. Presuming trustworthiness of another, give over responsibilities you can temporarily release.

> *One of the marvelous things about community is that it enables us to welcome and help people in a way we couldn't as individuals. When we pool our strength and share the work and responsibility, we can welcome many people, even those in deep distress, and perhaps help them find self-confidence and inner healing.* Jean Vanier, Philosopher, Writer, Humanitarian

Third – <u>Hold on to your self-care practices</u>

Challenging as it may be during times of duress, continue your best self-care practices. Exercise, walk, meditate, journal, continue your daily check-ins. Some may be unavoidably compromised. Do your best.

Fourth – <u>Consider professional help</u>

During times of overwhelming circumstances, we need to talk with someone. We need someone who has the tools to support and gently guide. At these times, we don't need advice-givers or fixers.

Following my dad's suicide and my wife's death, I participated in recovery/support groups. I needed help getting through these events and found it. There is comfort in being with others who have undergone similar challenging experiences, especially when facilitated by a trained professional.

If a loved one is experiencing challenge and difficulty, consider professional help for them. In the case of terminal illness, engage hospice early in the process; don't wait till the end is near. Hospice organizations offer expertise in palliative care, which is beneficial to the patient and the family. It pays to start earlier rather than later.

Fifth – Find the gift

Once your healing and recovery process has begun, find the gift in the event. Give this time. It will come when you're ready to receive it.

Your challenging experiences provide you with the foundation to be compassionate and supportive of others experiencing similar events. Use your experience to listen without fixing. Be a listening presence for a person in need of a compassionate ear.

You have survived the unthinkable. Stand with others who are also experiencing a life-tragedy.

If we climb high enough, we will reach a height from which tragedy will cease to look tragic. Irvin D. Yalom, psychiatrist, author, *When Nietzsche Wept*

CHAPTER 6

SHARE

We either share, or we hoard.

Where there is a lack of circulation in your home or office, the air becomes stale. Where there is a lack of circulation of fresh water in a pool or a pond, the water becomes stagnant. We must inhale, and we must exhale. Circulation – receiving and giving are part of the natural flow of life.

> **Your home is living space, not storage space.** Francine Jay, *Miss Minimalist, A Beautiful Life with Less Stuff*

There are many ways to share. Use them all. Share encouragement; give the gift of your support to others with joy and enthusiasm. Give all you can. Be a cheerleader for those sharing their dreams and their desire for a better life. Avoid pointing out the challenges they will encounter. Instead, encourage them to hold their vision and welcome it in their lives.

Be generous with your praise. "Nicely done." "Good job." "I like that." "You can do this." Such praise lifts and encourages. It only takes a few seconds. You can do this.

> *A kind gesture can reach a wound that only compassion can heal.*
> Steve Mariboli, author and speaker

A current trend for young kids are light- up shoes that flash as they walk. The next time you see a young person wearing a pair, tell them how much you like their shoes. "Wow, I really like your shoes!" Are they new?" Then smile and move on. You will have made a child happy.

Share your ears. Be a listener. Really listen to become part of the teller's story.

Listen to understand, not to comment, not to advise, not to judge. Just listen. We receive great benefit by "talking it out." We need a sincere listener to do so. Share your ears.

Be generous with your money. Create a space for giving in your budget. "But I can't afford to!" Really? I'm not suggesting you give it all away or deprive yourself or your family of basic needs. Give to the source of your spiritual food; donate to the spiritual/religious organizations that provide you with instruction, support, and community.

Find a way to circulate your money with those who are in need. A food pantry would be a start. Give regularly. Give anonymously. The people you help may never know it was you who provided their family with a meal. But you'll have an awareness that someone's life has been made better through your generosity.

> According to John Bunyan, English writer, and Puritan teacher, *"You have not lived today until you have done something for someone who can never repay you."*

Share yourself. Talk with others, converse with strangers. Don't worry that they might "take it the wrong way." Just be yourself, be generous with your uplifting thoughts. You'll feel better and hopefully; they will too.

Life is like cooking – if we understand the purpose of the ingredients, then we can make anything. Generosity, sharing, giving, are all ingredients of a purpose-filled life - a rich life. Cook up a good one by sharing.

> *Life is for loving, sharing, learning, smiling, caring, forgiving, laughing, hugging, and even more loving. I choose to live life this way. I want to live my life in such a way that when I get out of bed in the morning, the devil says, 'aw shit, he's up!* Steve Mariboli,

One cannot go through life like a ballplayer with a catcher's mitt on both hands. Give of your time, your talent, your treasure. Seek no reward for your generosity. There is no post-giving reward system for the giver. Giving something today does not mean some universal power will reward you by bestowing favor upon you sometime in the future. Being generous today, with no strings attached, means you will experience the reward associated with being generous today. That's it, and that's enough.

CHAPTER 7

DEVELOP YOUR RECEPTIVITY

> *Until we can receive with an open heart, we're never really giving with an open heart. When we attach judgment to receiving help, we knowingly or unknowingly attach judgment to giving help.* Brene Brown, *The Gifts of Imperfection*

How would you respond if you were approached with praise regarding your manner of dress? "OMG! That outfit is you! You look fantastic!" What would occur in your body as the compliments flowed your way? Healthy pride? Confidence? Embarrassment? Uneasiness?

And, how would you respond verbally? Would you fully accept the praise with a response such as, "Thanks! I too absolutely love the way it looks and feels on me. Thanks again!" or in your embarrassment or uneasiness, deflect the praise with comments such as, "Oh this, I got it at a bargain," or "Thanks, it's nothing special."

Let's take the experience of meeting another for lunch. Right at the start, your friend says, "Lunch is on me today. I'm so happy to spend time with you again." Is your response born of obligation? "OK, but I'll get the tip," or "Thanks, it's my turn next time?" Or is your response the ultimate statement of gratitude? "Thank you."

Do you experience a feeling of obligation or uneasiness when you receive a present, or perhaps an unexpected bounty of compliments or assistance of some form? Does gift receiving immediately evoke a response of "Gee, I didn't get them anything," or "How should I return the favor?"

Years ago, my former wife and I lived on a circular court. We knew our neighbors quite well. We had lived there for a number of years, never exchanging Christmas gifts with them. One year, she thought it a friendly gesture to send gifts to each of them, It didn't take long before the gifts started pouring into us. Some were rather costly.

The following year, we did not send nor receive any neighborly gifts. I'm wondering if in the previous year obligation was hard at work.

Our culture is rife with the idea that giving is morally superior to receiving. Some of our religious belief systems support that thinking. Such thinking creates a hierarchy of the giver being better than the receiver. How can that be?

Is it better to exhale than to inhale? Is the river flowing into a lake better than one flowing out? Is the person giving relief to natural disaster survivors really better than the survivors? Not in my mind. Both giving and receiving are equally necessary to sustain healthy circulation.

> *Gracious acceptance is an art - an art which most never bother to cultivate. We think that we have to learn how to give, but we forget about accepting things, which can be much harder than giving.... Accepting another person's gift is allowing him to express his feelings for you.*" Alexander McCall Smith, *Love Over Scotland*

We must unlearn that receiving either implies obligation or must be earned. Or that giving is "better" than receiving.

How can we live our life – really live it, if we are uncomfortable with receiving some of the most common gifts life offers such as compliments or cookies, or lunches, or neighborly Christmas gifts?

I'm also left wondering how we would ever place ourselves in a position to request help or assistance if we're uncomfortable with receiving it without feeling diminished.

> ***Always give without remembering and always receive without forgetting.***
> Brian Tracy, author, and speaker

While many avenues exist to change our thinking and create a greater degree of receptivity in our consciousness, I like to start with the simplest approach. I suggest each of you respond in a particular manner when given a gift, a freebie, or when good flows to you in any of the endless ways it may.

Simply say, "Thank you." No joking, no dismissing, no reciprocal remarks or acts, only "Thank you."

Become comfortable with receiving and accepting life's gifts without the need to deny, diminish, or reciprocate them. Respond with a simple "Thank you" and then enjoy what you've received.

Always choose thoughts that you are worthy and deserving of everything good coming your way.

And say "Thank you!"

CHAPTER 8

BE GRATEFUL

Be grateful for what you already have while you pursue your goals. If you aren't grateful for what you already have, what makes you think you would be happy with more. Roy T. Bennett, *The Light in the Heart*

It's common for businesses to take inventory on a regular basis. You've seen employees use scanners to tally up what's sitting on shelves. It's a necessary business practice to take stock of what you have.

Use that same technique in your expression of gratitude. Take a regular inventory of your life. Go through your entire house and look at everything. Really look. Take stock of the abundance you have around you.

Look at the pictures on the walls, the wonderful possessions you own and remember how you received them or who gave them to you. You live an incredibly blessed life. Choose to remind yourself of all you have and be grateful for it.

Look at the people who are in your life and give thanks for them. Give thanks for everything – not only the people who are in your life today but the people who have gone on before you.

Give thanks for those who founded the company you work for, your place of worship, the grocery store in which you shop, the cleaners you use. The list goes on and on. Be grateful.

> *In the end, though, maybe we must all give up trying to pay back the people in this world who sustain our lives. In the end, maybe it's wiser to surrender before the miraculous scope of human generosity and to just keep saying thank you, forever and sincerely, for as long as we have voices.* Elizabeth Gilbert, *Eat, Pray, Love; One woman's search for everything*

As you complete tasks listed on your calendar, write the word "grateful" after those you complete. You'll end up with a huge list of gratitude.

Placing the filter of gratitude on what we see and experience isn't Pollyanna-ish, it's realistic. It says, "I'm alive. Therefore I have the power to appreciate this, or do something about it, should I need to."

Gratitude is a great mind magnet since what we focus on and give energy to in our thoughts expands in our lives…as we are grateful…whatever we are grateful for becomes more plentiful in our lives.

The grateful heart draws itself to great things. The ungrateful heart, with a discouraged, complaining, covetous level of thought, will draw to itself limited things.

As we are appreciative and express gratitude, we attract more of what we appreciate.

Our time on earth is made up of moments, each one special. We weave together precious strands of time to create the fabric of our living. It is a miraculous journey we all share, this tapestry of human experience, for it is rich with the priceless offerings of relationships with all that we encounter.

Being gratefully aware of it all is the silken thread linking us to the finest miracle – the very privilege of being alive. Let us never forget, this journey is far too brief and fragile to let moments go by without acknowledging the wondrous gift we have been given.

Begin each day by giving thanks for what was yesterday and what will be today. And for the very "now moment," in which you are giving thanks.

> *Life and all it contains is totally gratuitous, 100% gift. I didn't bring myself into existence, nor is it I who keep myself going. I'm merely the recipient of this awesome gift. I didn't create the molecules of air I breathe in, nor the photons of light that strike my eye. it's all gift.* Father Ronald Stanley, a Catholic priest, associated with Rutgers University

CHAPTER 9

IT'S ALL ABOUT PERSPECTIVE

> *If you look the right way, you can see that the whole world is a garden.*
> Frances Hodgson Burnett, *The Secret Garden*

I'm standing at the shoreline, with one foot in the water, the other nestled in warm beach sand. As I look down the shoreline, I see the ever-changing marriage between the two: Quiet waves lapping at the wet sand, birds scurrying in and out across it, dark and light, regularly crossing a line in the sand. I have the experience of both worlds. Wet and dry.

I turn my head 90 degrees to one side and view only the water with shimmering diamonds dancing about the surface, reflecting off the ships that quietly ride to their unknown destination, ultimately disappearing from sight. I see children splashing and playing in the surf, hearing their shrill shrieks of delight. From this view, I only know the water, even though one foot is firmly anchored in the sand — only water.

I turn my head in the opposite direction. Now I gaze upon an endless row of skyscraper hotels, streams of glass ribbons flowing down their sides. I hear the sound of traffic; I see busy, noisy streets, somewhat shielded by clever landscaping, but there nevertheless. I see and experience only land, filled with concrete, glass, sound, and movement.

Three dramatically different perspectives, all gleaned from the same spot, simple head movements creating disparate views.

It's all a matter of perspective, which can be changed.

Quoting French writer, Marcel Proust, *"The only reality of discovery consists not in seeking new landscapes but in having new eyes."*

Our perspective has brought us the happiness and distress, success and failure, fear and love, we currently experience in life. I've previously stated that it's not what happens to us that matters, it's how we respond to what happens that creates our life experiences. It makes sense then, that our perspective, influencing our response, is the start of the experience.

We are in control of our perspective. Use it to grow. Do not use it to be bitter, resentful, angry, fearful, and the like. Use it to see possibilities.

The only reality that matters is one's perspective.

While in my car, I've backed out of the driveway to our home thousands of times, looking left and right, down the sidewalks, never seeing anyone who would be at risk. It reached the point that looking down the sidewalks seemed to provide the same useless information, so I pretty much ignored it. That was my perspective.

Which is why I opened my driver's side window, the other day, and apologized to a neighbor, whom I closely brushed as I backed out of my driveway. I didn't see what was standing (walking) directly to my side because my perspective was in the past.

I had formed an opinion in my mind of what I would see. I had formed my opinion based on the majority of my driveway experiences. Of course, that actually has nothing to do with what I may encounter the next time I back out.

Let's examine ourselves and ask, "Where in my life am I failing to see someone or something with new eyes? Where in my reality today, am I permitting worn evaluations, judgments, and histories to limit how I view those people and circumstances that I think I know well? How can I see this differently?" What would a change in my perspective bring to these circumstances?

What if we turned our heads just a few degrees and viewed relationships, employment, prosperity, our current life status from a new perspective? Why do we see only water or land, when both exist? And what about the sky? What new options and alternatives might we stumble upon with a new viewpoint?

> *Some people see the glass half full. Others see it half empty. I see a glass that's twice as big as it needs to be.* Comedian, George Carlin

And what if we continually turned our heads, exploring the entire panorama of possibilities when viewing ourselves? We are not the same person today that we were yesterday. We have an entire additional day of experiences that have reshaped us. The lessons we learned have changed us. The knowledge we have acquired guides us differently. Each day, our greater potential becomes more apparent. Why not see ourselves from the perspective of what's possible, instead of what we have accomplished?

Live your life, really live it. Live it with new eyes. There's always a new perspective to examine and entertain.

system navigation
55

CHAPTER 10

NO EXCUSES, STOP COMPLAINING

> *There is an expiry date on blaming your parents for steering you in the wrong direction; the moment you are old enough to take the wheel, responsibility lies with you.* J.K. Rowling, author of Harry Potter series

It's up to us. Whether it be a success or failure, winning or losing, happiness or sadness, the state of our relationships, our job, our health. It's all up to us. We may not always have control over the hand we are dealt, whether it be a large inheritance, or bankruptcy; perfect health or serious health challenge; the perfect neighbor or a total jerk; the job from heaven or the job from hell;

whatever hand we are dealt, we decide how we respond. We are in control of what we do about it.

No excuse that places responsibility for our life on someone else is good enough. It's our responsibility to determine what is ours to do to make it as right as we can make it. We must give up blaming, give up thinking that our present state of mind is "their" fault. It's our fault. It's up to us to make our lives the best we can. We change what we can change and adjust to what we cannot.

Give up complaining. I define complaining as whining and moaning about something without any intention of doing something about it. The problem isn't "out there," its right here, within us. If we're complaining, we are squandering a lot of precious time and energy on doing absolutely nothing about something that is bothersome to us, which makes no sense. Stop complaining and take action to change the circumstances.

If there's nothing we can do to change the circumstances, such as the weather, then stop moaning about it. I've heard it said, "It's not cold, you're just underdressed." Move on. Make the best of what currently is. Adjust. Isn't it a waste of life energy to whine about something over which we have no control?

> *What you're supposed to do when you don't like a thing is change it. If you can't change it, change the way you think about it. Don't complain.* Maya Angelou, *Wouldn't Take Nothing for My Journey Now*

Think about it. The more we revert to blame, the more we say that something else has to change for us to be happy. The more we say that we are responsible, the more we say that it's up to us, the more control we have over our life experiences. We don't have to wait for someone or something else to change; we can change. We have the power to make the best of it.

No excuses, stop blaming, stop complaining.

> *There's not a chance we'll reach our full potential until we stop blaming each other and start practicing personal accountability.* John Miller, QBQ: The Question Behind the Answer

CHAPTER 11

LET GO OF GUILT

> *Guilt is not a response to anger; it is a response to one's own actions or lack of action. If it leads to change then, it can be useful, since it is then no longer guilt but the beginning of knowledge. Yet all too often, guilt is just another name for impotence, for defensiveness destructive of communication; it becomes a device to protect ignorance and the continuation of things the way they are, the ultimate protection for changelessness.* Audre Lorde, *Sister Outsider: Essays and Speeches*

There's healthy guilt, and there's unhealthy guilt. When I say, "Let Go of Guilt," I mean the unhealthy kind.

There's the healthy guilt of self-reflection, self-examination in determining if change or an apology is necessary. Healthy guilt typically manifests as "I need to" statements. Such as: "I need to apologize for what I said," or "I need to change the way I think about this."

I define unhealthy guilt as a nagging undertow of critical remorse, typically triggered by something committed or omitted. This type of guilt lives in the shadowy background of our minds, often manifesting as a questioning tension in our gut, usually demonstrating as "I should" statements, such as, "I should attend the party, even though I don't like her," or "I should not have spoken up, now he's angry at me." Unhealthy guilt is self-judgment gone awry. It is defeating in nature. It is often rooted in our perception of how others might think about us.

This unhealthy guilt is a self-imposed sentence of blame, pronounced by a jury populated of our past failures. That is, a failure to meet someone else's mark or standard, or some cultural norm implanted in our psyche long ago by some outside authority determining who and what we should be and do. When we fail to meet this obsolete, externally imposed standard, we experience guilt.

When we operate from guilt, and something goes awry, we'll find difficulty in being authentic in our response. Why? Because we'll be operating from our perception of someone else's belief system of how we "should" be acting or responding.

It's far better to operate from our own rules.

> ***Calvin: There's no problem so awful, that you can't add some guilt to it and make it even worse.*** Bill Watterson, *The Complete Calvin, and Hobbes*

Guilt is harmful. It does not propel you forward; it holds you back in a quiet quagmire of shame and doubt. It's learned behavior, and it can be unlearned. When you notice it, ask yourself, "Whose voice am I hearing? Who is influencing me at this moment? Whose rules did I not follow?"

If it's not your voice, or your will, or your rules, redirect your thinking, change your focus, move on to something constructive, move your attention elsewhere.

If it is your voice, your will, your rules, make changes, make your amends and move on.

CHAPTER 12

IN CONCLUSION

> *We are the product of our past. We start each day where we left off the day before. Changing the way we dress, where we work and live, or even changing a name does not alter our basic constitution. Transformation of the self requires a radical alteration in the way that we perceive the world and derive meaning.* Kilroy J. Oldster, *Dead Toad Scrolls*

We are powerful beings. Our power is directed by means of our mind.

Our thinking creates our focus, and our focus leads us. To where? To where we are placing our attention.

Bring your attention to where you want to go.

Bring your attention to what you want.

Take action.

Live your life, really live it.

All the best to you,

Tom

ABOUT THE AUTHOR

Tom Wendt simply loves to help people "play more of the music that is within them." In his role as DreamBuilder Coach, he has helped scores of people move from procrastination to action, from self-doubt to sound decisions, and from fear to faith-in-action.

After a long and distinguished career at a large electric utility, at which he worked his way up from meter reader to regional dispatch superintendent, Tom left to pursue his dream of ministry.

Ordained in 2008, Tom grew a congregation of 30 to over 100, which ultimately purchased their own facility after leading them in a successful capital campaign. He says, "Although I was the spiritual leader, it took the entire congregation to make the move happen. It was heart-warming to watch congregants dream and work cooperatively."

He exited active ministry in 2016 and now devotes his time to inspirational speaking and life-coaching. His seminars, dealing with subjects such as stress, procrastination, decision-making, time management, building a better world, and more, consistently receive high praise as attendees make positive changes to their lives based on the tools for personal-growth and life-enrichment Tom provides.

Visit him at TheNextStepfor.me.

WORKSHOPS AND SEMINARS AVAILABLE FOR PRESENTATION

I love speaking to gatherings of all sizes and have been doing so for over four decades. I consider it a privilege to speak with groups of individuals wanting to draw from within themselves more of their wisdom, talent, courage, creativity, and other aspects of character. Here is a summary of my most popular seminars.

Speak Up! The Art of Initiating and Managing Difficult Conversations

An interactive personal-growth seminar

Learn to:

- Initiate and manage difficult conversations

- Listen from the heart in every situation

- Distinguish facts from stories in emotional situations

- Create a safe environment for dialogue

- Apply spiritual principles and Nonviolent Communications in daily communications

- Redirect conversations where dialogue has been lost

- Postpone Procrastination Now!

- Workshop benefits include:

- Removing the causes of procrastination

- Discerning the most important activities upon which to focus

- Gaining tools and techniques to lay aside procrastination and become a consistent producer

- Engaging in relaxing activities you love...guilt free

Here are just a few of the comments they're saying about the workshop:

- Interactive/was so interactive

- Simple exercises that don't take up much time – doable ways to get started

- So much wonderful material

- Great handouts and slides. Tom an excellent speaker

- Very well prepared! Loved the ideas and will definitely put them to use. Thank you!

- Concise, to the point, and very informative

Using Stress to Your Advantage

Participants will learn to:

- Assess levels of stress

- Identify signs and symptoms of stress overload

- Identify stress triggers (even positive events can be stressful)

- Manage stress by reducing the level of and incidences of stress

- Apply stress reduction techniques

Jump Start Your Life

The seminar will help you to:

- Quit trying harder – trying harder at what hasn't worked, doesn't work

- Ignore conventional approaches - "faith in the familiar" sets a trap

- Focus on the ends rather than the means – a vision is a must

- Make your move before you're ready – once underway, you'll know more than you know you know

- Look inside for the opportunity – you are your greatest asset

Build a Better World

My most interactive and inclusive seminar

Let's build a better world together

It's time for each of us to look at what is ours to do to build a better world

The Art of Making the Right Decisions

An interactive seminar

Have you ever made a decision you regretted? Have you ever decided to "wait" when the proper course was to take action? Have you ever taken immediate action when the proper course was to wait? Have you ever failed to make a decision when one was needed? My seminar will provide proven techniques to assist attendees in making the right decisions.

Create the Perfect Elevator Speech

An educational and interactive workshop

What you say in the first 30 seconds matters!

What Will You Do with Tomorrow?

An interactive and inclusive seminar

Have you ever found yourself wondering where the time has gone? How often do you think you're going to accomplish something tomorrow, but find that tomorrow never comes? Do you have any idea what you want your life to look like a year from now?

I look forward to hearing from you to discuss presentation dates and times.

Thank you for your interest.

TESTIMONIALS

"Tom has helped me find the focus and motivation to tackle obstacles I'd been fearful to face. His patient guidance gave me to confidence to approach these tasks in a no-nonsense manner and overcome them one by one. He has helped me grow and expand my business and continues to challenge me to reach greater heights. He has been a wonderful partner in my ongoing success!"

- Jeanne Cygnus, Cygnus Lactation Services, Mundelein, IL

"Working with a life coach can help bring clarity and focus to one's primary objectives while removing obstacles, real or imagined, that stand in the way of attaining them. Tom Wendt is a caring and insightful facilitator who brought resources and techniques to my awareness that helped me overcome obstacles at a critical point in my journey. I respect his work and enthusiastically recommend him to those looking to 'walk their talk' and live with greater integrity."

- John Hegner, Starbell, Harvard, IL.

Tom Wendt came to Unity Center of Clinton, Iowa, on two occasions to give a Sunday message and classes in the afternoon. Tom is always very thorough and well-prepared. He does careful research and provides excellent activities to go with the theme. I highly recommend any of his talks and classes. They are very practical with concepts you can put right to use in your own life.

Rev. Susan B. Peters, Clinton, IA

I had reached a point in my life where I knew there must be more to life but could not figure out how to get there. I realize now, I was searching for a more purposeful life which I am sure is why Tom Wendt came into my life. I was drawn to him because of his openness and sincere commitment to helping people. We started out just as buddies and eventually he became my life as well as business coach meeting on a weekly basis.

These weekly meeting have been going on now for over 5 years. Over those 5 years not only have I reached business goals that I thought we're unreachable, Tom's guidance has also helped me improve my family relationships as well as just leading a far more purposeful life.

I am grateful for Tom's guidance and look forward to many more years of weekly calls with Tom. My business and personal growth will continue to help me make a difference in this world! It's a gratifying feeling when you realize your true purpose and lead a life that's filling. For that I'll always be grateful to Tom.

Larry W. Sr., Huntley, IL

Last year in 2018 I was dealing with overwhelming negative drama from my extended family after the death of my mother. I just wanted to get past it all as there were dreaded family events coming up and Tom was extremely effective in guiding me through this difficult time. One of his common phrases is, 'Tell me what you want, not what you don't want!' No doubt I will continue to consult him with future challenges. Tom is the real deal!

-- **Karen S., Oak Park, IL.**

9 7 8 1 7 3 2 0 4 0 9 3 9